Chapter 1: Taking Charge - Your Budget Journey Begins

Imagine a world where your money works for you, instead of the other way around. A world where you're in control, making conscious choices about your finances, and feeling confident about the future. That's the power of a simple budget system.

Think of a budget as your personal roadmap to financial freedom. It helps you track your income and expenses, identify areas where you can save, and ultimately achieve your financial goals. Whether it's saving for a dream vacation, a comfortable retirement, or that perfect car, a budget is your key to unlocking those dreams.

This book is designed to be your friendly guide on this journey. We won't overwhelm you with complex financial jargon. Instead, we'll break down the budgeting process into simple, manageable steps. We'll focus on creating a system that's easy to understand, implement, and most importantly, stick to!

Why Budget?

Life throws a lot of curveballs. Unexpected expenses, medical bills, car repairs – they can all derail your financial plans. Budgeting helps you prepare for these bumps in the road. By understanding where your money goes each month, you can make informed decisions. You can avoid unnecessary spending and channel those funds towards your goals.

Benefits of Budgeting:

- **Peace of Mind:** Knowing exactly where your money stands eliminates financial stress and empowers you to make informed decisions.

- **Reaching Goals:** A budget helps you prioritize your spending and save towards specific goals, whether it's a down payment on a house or a dream vacation.

- **Debt Control:** Budgeting allows you to identify areas where you can cut back and free up money to pay down debt faster.

- **Planning for the Future:** By understanding your income and expenses, you can plan for emergencies, retirement, and other long-term goals.

Getting Started:

The first step is gathering your financial tools. You'll need:

- **Recent pay stubs:** This will help you determine your monthly income.

- **Bank statements:** This will show you where your money is currently going.

- **Pen and paper:** This is a great way to start tracking your expenses (or you can use a budgeting app or spreadsheet).

Next Steps:

In the coming chapters, we'll tackle these crucial aspects of budgeting:

- Calculating your income: Understanding your after-tax income is the foundation of your budget.

- Tracking your expenses: Identify where your money is currently going.

- Categorizing your spending: Break down your expenses into groups like rent, groceries, and entertainment.

- Creating a spending plan: Allocate your income towards needs, wants, and savings.

- Staying on track: Develop strategies to monitor your progress and adjust your budget as needed.

Remember, budgeting is a journey, not a destination. There will be adjustments along the way, but with commitment and a little effort, you'll be well on your way to achieving your financial goals!

Thoughts:

Financial Freedom for the Working Man: A Step-by-Step Guide

This book isn't about getting rich quick. It's about taking control of your finances, step-by-step. It's for the working man, the one who wants to bring order to their financial world, even if it takes time. My journey took over 5 years, and the first 3 were the hardest. Here's the key: discipline.

Track Your Income:

- Look at your income over the past 3 months and find the average.
- Any extra money after this average goes towards debt or investments.

Budgeting is Key, But Be Flexible:

- Budgeting is important, but it's a tool, not a rigid plan.
- Review your budget with each paycheck and adjust as needed. Keep moving forward!

Facing Tough Times:

- Feeling overwhelmed by a starter job and debt? Stay calm.
- Remember, "this too shall pass." You have the strength to manage your situation.

Invest in Yourself:

- If your starter job isn't ideal, focus on building your skills.
- It might take time, but this investment will pay off in the future.

Sacrifice for the Future You Want:

- Today's sacrifices pave the way for a better tomorrow.
- Visualize your dream life and use that vision as motivation.

Believe in Your Future:

- Positive affirmations work! Every morning, remind yourself of your future wealth.
- The Law of Attraction is real. Many people have overcome challenges and built the life they desired.

Open Mind and Empathy:

- Be open to new ideas and strategies as you progress.
- Show compassion for yourself throughout this journey to financial freedom.

This is Your Journey:

- I'm not here to sell you a dream. I'm here to teach you the discipline and methods that will brighten your future.
- Welcome aboard! I wish you all the best on your journey.

Chapter 2: Know Thyself - Understanding Your Income and Expenses

Congratulations! You've taken the first step towards financial freedom by gathering your financial tools. Now, let's delve deeper and understand the two sides of the financial coin: your income and your expenses.

Income: The Foundation

Consider your income the foundation of your budget. It's the money coming in that fuels your financial engine. To build a strong budget, you need to understand exactly how much income you have available each month.

Here's how to calculate your income:

1. Gather your recent pay stubs: Look for your after-tax income. This is the amount of money you receive after deductions for taxes, social security, and other contributions have been taken out.

2. Include all income sources: If you have additional income streams, like freelance work, side hustles, or rental income, include them in your calculation.

3. Average if income is inconsistent: If your income fluctuates month-to-month (like with commission-based jobs), calculate an average over the past few months to get a more realistic picture.

Expenses: Where Does Your Money Go?

Now, let's shine a light on the other side of the coin – your expenses. These are the outflows of money that need to be managed within your income limits.

Here's how to get a good grasp on your expenses:

1. Review your bank statements: Trace a few months of statements, noting down every single expense. Don't worry, you don't need to memorize every detail – just categorize them for now.

2. Gather receipts: If you tend to use cash or forget to record expenses, keep your receipts for a month to get a more accurate picture.

3. Be honest: Don't underestimate or downplay your spending.

Categorizing Your Expenses

Once you have a list of your expenses, let's organize them into categories. This helps you understand where your money is truly going. Here are some common expense categories:

- Fixed expenses: These are essential expenses that remain relatively constant each month, like rent, utilities, car payments, and loan payments.
- Variable expenses: These expenses can fluctuate from month to month, such as groceries, dining out, entertainment, and transportation.
- Debt payments: Include all your minimum debt payments here.
- Savings: This is where you want to allocate a portion of your income for future goals.

Now, categorize all your expenses under these headings. You can further refine them if needed (e.g., groceries vs. dining out within variable expenses).

Analyzing Your Spending

Once categorized, take a good look at your expenses. Are there any surprises? Are there areas where you can cut back?

This is not about depriving yourself, but about being mindful of where your money goes. Perhaps you can find cheaper grocery alternatives, cook more at home instead of eating out frequently, or downsize your cable package. Every little bit saved counts!

The Takeaway

By understanding your income and categorizing your expenses, you've laid the groundwork for creating a realistic and achievable budget.

In the next chapter, we'll take this understanding further and delve into creating a spending plan that allocates your income towards your needs, wants, and most importantly, your financial goals!

Survival Mode: Prioritizing Needs on a Tight Budget

When my income wasn't enough to cover everything, I had to prioritize ruthlessly. Here are the 3 essentials that must be covered, even if everything else needs to wait:

1. **Shelter (60-70% of income):** Rent or mortgage comes first. Look for places with utilities included.
2. **Transportation (20-30% of income):** You need a reliable car to get to work and find new opportunities. Consider gas mileage and budget accordingly.
3. **Communication (5-10% of income):** A basic phone plan (around $50) is essential to stay connected. Look for budget-friendly options through third-party sellers.

Remember: These are your non-negotiables. Once these are covered, you can re-evaluate other expenses.

When Life Throws Curveballs: Prioritize, Adapt, and Plan

Life can get tough. Sometimes, everything seems to fall apart at once. Here's what to do:

Focus on Essentials:

- Prioritize your needs. Food, shelter, and basic necessities come first.
- Don't be afraid to seek temporary assistance from food banks or soup kitchens.
- Remember, this is just temporary. When things turn around, pay it forward by helping others in need.

Short-term Hustle, Long-term Vision:

- A second job might be necessary in the short term.
- But keep your long-term goals in mind. Don't get stuck in a two-job rut for a decade.

Invest in Yourself:

- Use this time to build valuable skills. This is an investment in your future.
- Don't get complacent in a starter job that won't get you where you want to be.

Remember: Working a basic job for years won't achieve your dreams. Take action and develop the skills needed for success.

Chapter 3: Building Your Budget Castle - Creating a Spending Plan

Welcome back, budget warrior! Now that you have a firm grasp on your income and expenses, it's time to build the castle of your financial future – your spending plan.

Think of a spending plan as a roadmap that allocates your income towards various needs and goals. This plan will guide your spending decisions and ensure you're on track to achieve your financial aspirations.

The Pillars of Your Spending Plan:

Your spending plan will rest on three main pillars:

1. Needs: These are essential expenses you can't live without, like housing, utilities, groceries, transportation, and minimum debt payments.
2. Wants: These are things you desire but can live without, like entertainment, dining out, and subscriptions.
3. Savings: This is the crucial pillar that fuels your future goals, like a down payment on a house, retirement savings, or that dream vacation.

Building the Framework:

Here's how to create your spending plan:

1. Prioritize Needs: List out all your essential expenses. These take top priority in your budget.
2. Estimate Needs Cost: Based on your bank statements and recent bills, estimate the average monthly cost for each essential expense.
3. Factor in Wants: Now, list your wants. Be honest! But remember, wants don't get the same priority as needs.
4. Estimate Wants Cost: Estimate the average monthly cost for each want.
5. Savings Goal: Determine your desired savings amount each month. This could be a fixed amount or a percentage of your income.

6. Total it Up: Add up the estimated costs for all your needs, wants, and desired savings amount.

Balancing the Budget:

Now comes the balancing act. Here's where your income comes into play.

- Ideal Scenario: If your total expenses (needs + wants + savings) are less than your income, congratulations! You have wiggle room to allocate more towards savings or increase your wants allocation slightly.

- Reality Check: More likely, your total expenses will be close to or exceed your income. Here's where adjustments come in.

Making Adjustments:

If your expenses are exceeding your income, it's time to make some adjustments:

- Review Wants: Look for areas where you can cut back on wants. Can you reduce dining out, find cheaper entertainment options, or temporarily suspend subscriptions?

- Negotiate: Can you negotiate lower rates for essentials like cable or internet?

- Increase Income: Are there ways to increase your income, like taking on a side hustle or negotiating a raise?

Remember: This is an iterative process. Don't get discouraged if you need to adjust your plan throughout the month or as your circumstances change. The key is to be flexible and stay committed.

Tracking Your Progress:

Once you've finalized your spending plan, it's crucial to track your progress. There are various methods:

- Pen and Paper: This is a simple and classic option. Note down your actual expenses and compare them to your budgeted amounts.

- Budgeting Apps: Several budgeting apps can help you track your spending, categorize expenses, and stay on track.

- Spreadsheets: Create a spreadsheet to track your income and expenses and visualize your progress with charts and graphs.

The Power of Consistency:

Building a successful budget is a marathon, not a sprint. Consistency is key. By diligently tracking your progress and making adjustments where necessary, you'll be well on your way to achieving your financial goals.

In the next chapter, we'll explore strategies to help you stay motivated and stick to your budget, even when faced with temptations or unexpected expenses.

Facing Reality and Building Resilience: The Road to Freedom

Let's be honest: living paycheck to paycheck is a harsh reality for many. One unexpected event can feel like the world is caving in. But here's the good news: you're not alone, and change is possible.

Taking Control: Hard Choices, Clear Paths

The road to financial freedom requires tough decisions. But with the right tools, like a well-defined budget, you can map your progress and see your path to a brighter future.

Discipline is Your Ally

There will be bumps along the road. But with discipline and willpower, you can overcome these challenges.

Support System Matters

Having a partner on your side, a cheerleader (family or friend), makes a world of difference. Discussing your budget goals and tracking progress together strengthens your resolve.

Embrace the Grind: Budgeting for the Worst

Remember those times hunched over a pen and paper, meticulously crafting your budget? It might not have been glamorous, but it was crucial.

My Secret Weapon: Worst-Case Scenario Planning

Here's a powerful tip: factor in "worst-case scenarios" when building your budget. This way, unexpected events become bumps, not roadblocks. Adjust as needed, but be prepared.

The Power of Progress

As you build your emergency fund, those budget adjustments become less frequent. You'll spend less time balancing the books and more time enjoying the peace of mind that financial security brings.

Remember: Change is possible. With the right tools, support system, and a spirit of resilience, you can conquer the paycheck-to-paycheck cycle and build a brighter financial future.

Chapter 4: Conquering the Dragons - Staying Motivated and on Track

Congratulations! You've built the foundation of your financial future – a solid spending plan. Now, let's equip you with the tools to slay the dragons that might try to derail your budgeting journey – temptations, unexpected expenses, and moments of discouragement.

Staying Motivated:

Motivation is the fuel that keeps your budgeting engine running. Here are some tips to stay fired up:

- Visualize Your Goals: Keep your financial dreams at the forefront of your mind. Create a vision board, set a screensaver with your dream car (or vacation!), or write down your goals and post them somewhere you'll see them daily.

- Celebrate Milestones: Reaching budgeting milestones, big or small, deserves a pat on the back! Did you stick to your grocery budget for a month? Celebrate with a low-cost reward like a movie night in.

- Find a Budgeting Buddy: Partnering with a friend or family member who's also budgeting can be a great source of encouragement and accountability. You can share tips, motivate each other, and celebrate successes together.

- Track Your Progress: Seeing your progress visually can be incredibly motivating. Use charts, graphs, or simply tick marks on a calendar to track your spending and savings goals. Seeing the progress you've made reinforces your commitment.

Taming Unexpected Expenses:

Life throws curveballs. Unexpected expenses can throw your budget off track. Here's how to be prepared:

- **Build an Emergency Fund:** Aim to save 3-6 months of living expenses in an emergency fund. This safety net will help you cover unexpected costs without derailing your budget.
- **Review Your Budget Regularly:** Revisit your budget every month or two. Adjust for any changes in income or expenses to ensure it remains realistic and effective.
- **Be Flexible:** Unexpected expenses don't have to derail your entire budget. Review your spending plan and see if you can temporarily reduce spending in other areas to compensate for the unexpected cost.

Slaying Temptation:

Temptation is a constant foe in the budgeting battle. Here are some strategies to overcome it:

- **The 24-Hour Rule:** Before making an impulse purchase, wait 24 hours. Often, the urge to buy fades with time.
- **The Needs vs. Wants Test:** Ask yourself, "Is this a need or a want?" Prioritize needs in your spending, and if it's a want, consider if it aligns with your long-term goals.
- **Find Alternatives:** Craving a night out? Explore cheaper alternatives like a movie night at home or a picnic in the park.

Remember: Everyone makes mistakes. If you slip up and overspend, don't beat yourself up. Just get back on track with your next paycheck. Consistency is key!

Building Long-Term Habits:

Budgeting isn't just about numbers; it's about building healthy financial habits. Here are some tips:

- **Automate Savings:** Set up automatic transfers to your savings account each payday. This "pay yourself first" approach ensures you prioritize saving.
- **Review Your Spending Regularly:** Regularly review your bank statements and categorize your expenses. This helps you identify areas for improvement and track your progress towards your goals.
- **Make Budgeting a Habit:** Integrate budgeting into your routine. Set aside a specific time each week or month to review your plan and track your progress.

By following these tips and staying committed, you'll transform budgeting from a chore into a powerful tool that empowers you to take control of your finances and achieve your financial dreams!

Notes:

Chapter 5: Your Budget Toolkit - Streamlining Your Financial Journey

Congratulations! You've conquered the foundational aspects of budgeting. Now, let's delve into some practical tips and tricks to make your budgeting journey smoother, faster, and more efficient. Consider this chapter your personal budgeting toolkit!

Finding the Right Tools:

The right tools can make a big difference in your budgeting success. Here are some options to consider:

- Budgeting Apps: Many budgeting apps offer features like expense tracking, automatic categorization, goal setting, and bill reminders. Explore free and paid options to find one that suits your needs and preferences.

- Spreadsheets: For those comfortable with spreadsheets, creating a customized budget template can be a powerful tool. You can personalize categories, track progress with charts, and automate calculations.

- The Classic Pen and Paper: This simple method is still effective. Keep a notebook specifically for tracking income and expenses. It's low-tech but allows for flexibility and customization.

Simplifying Your Spending:

- **Embrace Automation:** Set up automatic payments for recurring bills to avoid late fees and ensure timely payments. Consider automatic transfers to your savings account to ensure you "pay yourself first."

- **Utilize Cash Envelopes (Optional):** If you struggle with impulse purchases, allocating specific amounts of cash for different spending categories (groceries, entertainment) can be helpful. Once the cash runs out, the spending stops for that category until the next budgeting cycle.

Meal Planning and Grocery Hacks:

- **Plan Your Meals:** Plan your meals for the week and create a grocery list based on your plan. This helps avoid impulse purchases and food waste.

- **Utilize Coupons and Discounts:** Look for coupons online, in newspapers, or apps. Take advantage of store loyalty programs and discount grocery stores.

- **Cook More at Home:** Eating out can significantly impact your budget. Cooking at home is generally cheaper and healthier.

- **Explore Free Activities:** Many libraries, parks, and community centers offer free events, workshops, and activities. Take advantage of these for entertainment and socializing.

- **Consider Alternatives:** Instead of expensive movies or concerts, explore cheaper options like movie nights at home, game nights with friends, or free outdoor concerts.Remember: Budgeting is a journey, not a destination. There will be adjustments along the way, but with these tools and a positive mindset, you'll be well on your way to achieving your financial goals!Bonus Tip: Reward yourself for achieving milestones! Celebrate your budgeting successes, big or small. This reinforces positive financial habits and keeps you motivated on your journey.

Chapter 6: Beyond the Basics - Budgeting for Life's Milestones

Congratulations! You've mastered the fundamentals of budgeting and are well on your way to taking control of your finances. Now, let's explore how to adapt your budgeting skills to navigate some of life's major milestones.

Life throws financial curveballs, and being prepared with a flexible budget is key. Here's how to budget for some common milestones:

1. Handling Debt:

- Prioritize High-Interest Debt: Focus on paying off high-interest debt (credit cards, payday loans) first. Consider strategies like the debt snowball or avalanche method to accelerate your debt payoff journey.

- Negotiate Interest Rates: If possible, try to negotiate lower interest rates on your existing debt.

- Increase Debt Payments: Once you have some wiggle room in your budget, consider allocating additional funds towards debt payments to eliminate debt faster.

2. Saving for a Down Payment:

- Set a Savings Goal: Determine the amount you need for a down payment on a house. Factor in closing costs and other associated fees.

- Increase Savings Contributions: Review your budget and see where you can increase your savings contributions towards your down payment goal.

- Explore Government Programs: Depending on your location, there might be government programs offering assistance with down payments for first-time homebuyers.

3. Planning for a Wedding:

- Set a Realistic Budget: Discuss financial expectations with your partner and set a realistic budget for the wedding.

- Prioritize Spending: Identify the most important aspects of your wedding (venue, food, photography) and allocate your budget accordingly. Explore cost-saving alternatives for other areas.

- Consider Alternative Funding: Explore crowdfunding options or contributions from family to help cover some wedding costs.

4. Budgeting for Children:

- Estimate Childcare Costs: Research childcare options and factor in associated costs into your budget.

- Start Saving Early: The earlier you start saving for your child's future education, the better. Utilize college savings plans or investment accounts.

- Adjust Your Budget: With a new addition to the family, your expenses will increase. Review your budget and adjust spending in other areas to accommodate these new costs.

5. Planning for Retirement:

- Start Early: The earlier you start saving for retirement, the more time your money has to grow through compound interest.

- Maximize Employer Contributions: If your employer offers a retirement savings plan with matching contributions, maximize your contributions to take full advantage of this benefit.

- Review Retirement Needs: Estimate your retirement needs and adjust your savings contributions accordingly.

Remember: These are just general guidelines. Adapt your budgeting approach to your specific circumstances and financial goals.

The key takeaway is to be proactive and plan for life's milestones. By incorporating these budgeting strategies, you can ensure you're financially prepared for whatever life throws your way.

Congratulations! You've completed this guide to budgeting. With dedication and the tools you've learned, you can achieve your financial goals and build a secure and prosperous future for yourself!

Chapter 7: The Road to Financial Freedom

Congratulations! You've reached the end of this guide, but the beginning of your financial journey. You've equipped yourself with the knowledge and tools to build a solid budget, manage your finances effectively, and achieve your financial goals.

Remember, budgeting is a continuous process. Regularly review your budget, adapt it to changing circumstances, and celebrate your milestones. Here are some parting thoughts:

- Embrace the Journey: Budgeting is not a chore, but a path to financial freedom. Enjoy the process of taking control of your finances and making informed decisions about your money.

- Be Patient: Building financial security takes time and consistent effort. Don't get discouraged by setbacks. Learn from them and keep moving forward.

- Seek Help: If you need additional support, there are many resources available. Consider consulting a financial advisor, budgeting apps, or online budgeting communities.

- Share Your Knowledge: Help others embark on their financial journeys. Share your budgeting success stories and encourage others to take control of their finances.

By putting these principles into practice, you'll be well on your way to achieving financial security and building a bright future. Remember, the power is in your hands!

Option 2: Appendix - Budgeting Resources

Appendix: Budgeting Resources

This appendix serves as a resource guide to help you further your budgeting journey:

Building a Secure Future: Automate Your Savings and Grow Your Wealth

Saving for retirement can feel overwhelming, especially on a tight budget. Here are some strategies to make saving easier and more impactful:

Automate Your Savings:

- Utilize your employer's 401(k) savings plan. This automates contributions, taking the money out of your paycheck before you even see it.
- You can still access these funds in an emergency through a hardship loan, but use this option only for critical situations as it can set back your retirement goals.

Double Benefit: Tax Advantages:

- Contributing to a 401(k) reduces your taxable income, meaning you keep more of your hard-earned money. This is essentially a tax break that incentivizes retirement savings.

Invest Wisely:

- Review the investment options within your 401(k) plan. Choose a portfolio that aligns with your risk tolerance and long-term goals.
- Don't be afraid to shop around for a low-cost provider to manage your 401(k) fees. Keeping fees low helps maximize your returns.

Bonus Tip:

- As your income grows, consider gradually increasing your 401(k) contribution percentage. This will accelerate your wealth accumulation over time.

By automating your savings, taking advantage of tax benefits, and investing wisely, you can build a secure financial future and achieve your retirement goals.

Appendix: Empower Your Financial Journey

This appendix serves as a resource guide to help you further your budgeting journey:

Books:

- **"The Richest Man in Babylon" by George S. Clason:** This classic book, which inspired the concepts in this guide, offers timeless wisdom on building wealth through budgeting, saving, and investing.
- **"I Will Teach You To Be Rich" by Ramit Sethi:** This practical guide provides actionable steps to manage your money, pay off debt, and build wealth.
- **"The Simple Path to Wealth" by J.L. Collins:** This straightforward book outlines a low-cost investment strategy for long-term financial success.

Websites:

- **National Endowment for Financial Education (https://www.nefe.org/)** This non-profit organization provides free educational resources on budgeting, saving, and investing.
- **Consumer Financial Protection Bureau (https://www.consumerfinance.gov/)** This government agency offers information and tools to help you make informed financial decisions.

Budgeting Apps:

- **Mint** (https://mint.intuit.com/) This free app helps you track your income and expenses, create budgets, and set financial goals.
- **You Need a Budget (YNAB)** (https://www.ynab.com/) (Subscription-based) This app uses a unique budgeting method to help you manage your money proactively.

Remember: This list is not exhaustive. Explore available resources to find what works best for you. By utilizing these resources and applying the budgeting principles outlined in this guide, you empower yourself to take control of your finances and build a future filled with financial security and peace of mind.

Chapter 8: Putting It All Together - The Richest Man in Babylon Meets the $20-an-Hour Earner

In the previous chapters, you've learned the fundamentals of budgeting and explored how to adapt it for different life stages. Now, let's bridge the gap between the timeless wisdom of "The Richest Man in Babylon" and the practical realities of someone earning $20 an hour.

The Richest Man in Babylon:

This classic book, written by George S. Clason, uses parables set in ancient Babylon to illustrate timeless financial principles. Here are some key takeaways that resonate with modern budgeting:

- **Pay Yourself First:** Just like the characters in the book who allocate a portion of their income towards savings, paying yourself first through automatic savings transfers is crucial for building wealth.

- Live Below Your Means: The Babylonians avoided unnecessary spending and lived within their means. Translating this to modern budgeting translates to prioritizing needs over wants and avoiding lifestyle inflation.
- Invest Wisely: The book emphasizes the importance of putting your money to work for you through sound investments. While the investment landscape has changed, the core principle of growing your wealth through investments remains relevant.

The $20-an-Hour Earner:

Earning $20 an hour translates to a pre-tax income of roughly $40,000 annually for a full-time job (assuming 40 hours a week). Here's how to apply budgeting principles to this scenario:

- Track Your Expenses: Just like the Babylonians who meticulously tracked their finances, understanding where your money goes is crucial.
- Create a Budget: Allocate your income towards essential expenses (rent, utilities, groceries), debt payments (if any), and savings. Aim to save at least 10% of your income, but adjust based on your financial goals.
- Find Savings Opportunities: Explore ways to reduce expenses, like cooking more at home, finding cheaper entertainment options, or negotiating bills. Every dollar saved is a dollar towards your goals.

Bridging the Gap:

The lessons from "The Richest Man in Babylon" are universally applicable. Regardless of your income, the principles of paying yourself first, living below your means, and using your money wisely are key to building financial security.

Here are some additional tips for the $20-an-Hour Earner:

- Develop Multiple Income Streams: Consider side hustles or freelance work to increase your income and accelerate your financial goals.
- Set SMART Financial Goals: Set Specific, Measurable, Achievable, Relevant, and Time-bound goals for your savings and investments.
- Seek Guidance: Free resources like government websites or budgeting apps can be invaluable tools. Consider consulting a financial advisor for personalized advice.

Remember: Building wealth takes time and consistent effort. The key is to start now, regardless of your income level. By applying the principles outlined in this chapter and throughout this guide, you'll be well on your way to achieving financial freedom, just like the Richest Man in Babylon.

Commit to Your Future: Invest Consistently and Learn

Building wealth is a marathon, not a sprint. Here's how to make consistent progress, no matter your starting point:

Pay Yourself First:

- Aim to invest at least 10% of your income, regardless of what life throws your way. This is your "untouchable" money, dedicated to your future self.
- If 10% feels overwhelming, start with a smaller amount and gradually increase it as your budget allows. Every little bit counts!

Become an Investment Student:

- The market may seem complex, but financial literacy is empowering. Understand the "why" behind everyday occurrences, like coffee prices or oil fluctuations. This knowledge will help you make informed investment decisions.
- Don't aim to be a master; a solid understanding is key.

Learning Can Be Fun!

- Find resources that make learning about investing enjoyable. Join online forums, attend workshops, or listen to podcasts. You're not alone!
- Even as I write this, I'm constantly seeking new knowledge to refine my investment strategies and secure my financial future.

Remember:

- Consistency is key. Invest regularly, even if it's a small amount.
- Knowledge is power. Educate yourself to become a smarter investor.
- Enjoy the journey! Learning about finance can be fascinating.

By following these steps, you'll be well on your way to building long-term wealth and achieving your financial goals.

Notes:

Chapter 9: Conquering the High-Cost Climb - Strategies for Low Wages in a Pricey World

Living in a world with a high cost of living while earning a low wage can feel like a constant uphill battle. But fear not, budget warrior! This chapter equips you with strategies to navigate this challenging terrain and achieve financial stability.

Understanding the Landscape:

The high cost of living can encompass essentials like housing, transportation, and groceries. Here are some initial steps:

- **Calculate Your True Cost of Living:** Go beyond basic needs. Factor in transportation costs if you rely on public transport, childcare expenses if applicable, and any other essential costs specific to your situation.
- **Identify Areas for Adjustment:** Review your spending and categorize your expenses. Look for areas where you can potentially cut back without compromising your well-being.

Strategies for Stretching Your Dollar:

- **Embrace Budgeting:** A well-crafted budget becomes your roadmap to financial survival. Track your income and expenses to identify areas for improvement.
- **Prioritize Needs Over Wants:** Distinguish between essential needs and fleeting desires. Allocate your limited resources towards essential expenses first.
- **Negotiate Bills:** Don't be afraid to negotiate with service providers like cable companies or internet providers. You might be surprised at the potential savings.
- **Explore Cost-Saving Alternatives:** Embrace cheaper alternatives for essentials. Consider generic brands for groceries, explore public transportation options, or find free or low-cost entertainment options (libraries, parks, community events).

Boosting Your Income:

- **Increase Your Earning Potential:** Consider upskilling or taking on additional certifications to potentially qualify for higher-paying jobs within your field.
- **Explore Side Hustles:** The gig economy offers flexibility. Look for freelance work, online opportunities, or part-time jobs that complement your schedule and skills.
- **Sell Unused Items:** De-clutter your belongings. Sell unwanted items online or at garage sales to generate some extra cash.

Seeking Assistance:

There's no shame in seeking help. Here are some resources that can offer support:

- **Government Assistance Programs:** Explore government programs that offer rental assistance, food stamps, or utility subsidies depending on your location and eligibility.
- **Non-Profit Organizations:** Many non-profit organizations provide financial counseling, budgeting assistance, or even food pantries to those in need.

Building Financial Resilience:

- **Emergency Fund:** Even with a limited income, aim to build a small emergency fund to cover unexpected expenses and avoid falling deeper into debt.

- Long-Term Goals: Don't lose sight of your long-term financial goals, like saving for a down payment on a house or future education. Even small, consistent savings can make a difference.

Remember: The key is to be proactive and resourceful. By implementing these strategies and remaining committed to your financial goals, you can navigate the challenges of a high cost of living and build a brighter financial future.

Bonus Tip: Embrace a frugal mindset. Frugality isn't about deprivation, but about making conscious choices and maximizing the value of your money. Look for ways to live a fulfilling life without breaking the bank!

Your Thoughts:

Chapter 11: Investing for the Future - Building Wealth with Small Steps

Congratulations! You've mastered the art of budgeting and are well on your way to managing your day-to-day finances effectively. Now, let's explore how to put your savings to work for you and build wealth for the long term through smart investing.

This chapter dives into two specific strategies: regular investing in dividend-paying stocks and utilizing a 529 plan for education savings.

Investing 101:

Investing involves using your money to purchase assets that have the potential to grow in value over time. There are various investment options, each with its own risk-reward profile.

Dividend Investing:

Dividend-paying stocks are a popular option for beginners. These companies share a portion of their profits with shareholders through regular dividend payments. While stock prices can fluctuate, dividend payments provide a steady stream of income.

Investing $20 a Day:

Investing $20 a day might seem like a small amount, but the power of compound interest can work wonders over time. Here's the idea:

- Compound interest allows your earnings to generate additional earnings.
- Regularly investing small amounts allows you to benefit from compounding over the long term.

Important Considerations:

- Do Your Research: Before investing in any stock, research the company, its financial health, and its dividend history.
- Diversification: Don't put all your eggs in one basket. Diversify your investments across different sectors and asset classes to mitigate risk.
- Long-Term Focus: The stock market can be volatile in the short term. Focus on a long-term investment horizon to ride out market fluctuations and benefit from potential growth.

There are several ways to invest $20 a day:

- Fractional Shares: Some brokerage firms allow you to purchase fractional shares of stocks, enabling you to invest smaller amounts in high-priced stocks.
- Micro-Investing Apps: These apps allow you to invest small amounts regularly and often automate the process.

Remember: Investing involves inherent risks. This is not a get-rich-quick scheme.

529 Plans - Saving for Education:

A 529 plan is a tax-advantaged savings account specifically designed for education expenses. Here are the key benefits:

- Tax Advantages: Contributions to a 529 plan may be tax-deductible in your state, and earnings grow tax-free when used for qualified education expenses.

- Flexibility: 529 plans can be used for various qualified education expenses, including tuition, fees, books, and even room and board.

Even small, regular contributions to a 529 plan can accumulate significantly over time, thanks to tax advantages and potential compound interest.

Important Considerations:

- State Plans: Each state offers its own 529 plan with varying features and benefits. Research your state's plan or consider plans from other states with favorable features.

- Investment Options: Most 529 plans offer a variety of investment options with different risk-reward profiles. Choose an option that aligns with your investment goals and time horizon.

Investing $20 a Day + 529 Plans:

While $20 a day might seem small, consistently investing this amount in dividend stocks and a 529 plan can be a powerful way to build wealth for your future and your children's education.

Remember: Consult with a financial advisor for personalized investment advice tailored to your specific circumstances and risk tolerance.

The key takeaway is to start early and invest consistently, even with small amounts. By taking these steps, you'll be well on your way to achieving your long-term financial goals!

Chapter 12: Retirement Rumble: 401(k) vs. Traditional IRA vs. Roth IRA

Choosing the right retirement account is a crucial decision that can significantly impact your future financial security. This chapter throws down the gauntlet in the battle between three common retirement accounts: the 401(k), the Traditional IRA, and the Roth IRA.

The Contenders:

1. 401(k): An employer-sponsored retirement plan that allows you to contribute pre-tax salary towards your retirement savings. Many employers offer matching contributions, essentially free money to boost your retirement savings.

2. Traditional IRA: An individual retirement account that allows you to contribute pre-tax income or deduct your contributions from your taxable income. Earnings on contributions grow tax-deferred, but withdrawals in retirement are taxed as ordinary income.

3. Roth IRA: An individual retirement account funded with after-tax dollars. Contributions don't grow tax-deferred, but qualified withdrawals in retirement are generally tax-free.

The Match Game:

A significant advantage of a 401(k) is the potential for employer matching contributions. This is essentially free money that boosts your retirement savings. If your employer offers a match, prioritize contributing enough to your 401(k) to maximize the match.

Taxation Throwdown:

- Traditional IRA: Contributions are typically tax-deductible, lowering your current taxable income. However, withdrawals in retirement are taxed as ordinary income.

- Roth IRA: Contributions are made with after-tax dollars, so they don't lower your current taxable income. However, qualified withdrawals in retirement are generally tax-free, including both contributions and earnings.

Choosing Your Champion:

The best retirement account for you depends on your current tax bracket and your projected tax bracket in retirement.

- If you're in a lower tax bracket now and expect to be in a higher tax bracket in retirement, a Roth IRA might be a good choice. You'll pay taxes on your contributions now, but your withdrawals in retirement will be tax-free.

- If you're in a higher tax bracket now and expect to be in a lower tax bracket in retirement, a Traditional IRA might be a better option. You'll get a tax break on your contributions now, but you'll pay taxes on your withdrawals in retirement.

Additional Considerations:

- Income Limits: There are income limits for contributing to Roth IRAs. You can still contribute to a Traditional IRA and convert those contributions to a Roth IRA later (subject to taxes and income limitations).

- Investment Options: 401(k) plans typically offer a limited selection of investment options compared to IRAs.

Remember: Consult with a financial advisor to discuss your specific situation and determine which retirement account best aligns with your long-term financial goals.

Bonus Tip: You can leverage both accounts! Contribute to your 401(k) to maximize employer matching and then consider opening a Roth IRA to diversify your retirement savings and potentially benefit from tax-free withdrawals in retirement.

By understanding the key differences between these retirement accounts and considering your tax situation, you can choose the champion that will help you achieve a secure and prosperous retirement!

Building a Secure Future: Automate Your Savings and Grow Your Wealth

Saving for retirement can feel overwhelming, especially on a tight budget. Here are some strategies to make saving easier and more impactful:

Automate Your Savings:

- Utilize your employer's 401(k) savings plan. This automates contributions, taking the money out of your paycheck before you even see it.
- You can still access these funds in an emergency through a hardship loan, but use this option only for critical situations as it can set back your retirement goals.

Double Benefit: Tax Advantages:

- Contributing to a 401(k) reduces your taxable income, meaning you keep more of your hard-earned money. This is essentially a tax break that incentivizes retirement savings.

Invest Wisely:

- Review the investment options within your 401(k) plan. Choose a portfolio that aligns with your risk tolerance and long-term goals.
- Don't be afraid to shop around for a low-cost provider to manage your 401(k) fees. Keeping fees low helps maximize your returns.

Bonus Tip:

- As your income grows, consider gradually increasing your 401(k) contribution percentage. This will accelerate your wealth accumulation over time.

By automating your savings, taking advantage of tax benefits, and investing wisely, you can build a secure financial future and achieve your retirement goals.

Notes:

Chapter 13: Building Your Financial Empire Together - Life Partner Goals for Financial Freedom

Congratulations! You've conquered budgeting basics, explored investment strategies, and are well on your way to achieving financial security. Now, let's delve into the exciting world of building a financially secure future with your life partner.

Communication is Key:

Financial compatibility is a crucial element of a healthy relationship. Open and honest communication about finances is essential for setting joint financial goals and navigating your financial journey together.

Discuss Your Financial Past and Present:

- Be transparent: Share your financial history, including debt, income, and spending habits.

- Understand each other's financial goals: Do you dream of early retirement, owning a vacation home, or financial independence?

- Discuss your financial comfort levels: Are you a spender or a saver? How comfortable are you with debt or risk?

Crafting Your Financial Masterplan:

Once you have a clear understanding of each other's financial situation and goals, it's time to create a joint financial plan. Here's what to consider:

- Joint Budget: Create a comprehensive budget that incorporates both your incomes and expenses.

- Shared Financial Goals: Set joint financial goals, from saving for a dream vacation to planning for retirement.

- Debt Management: Develop a plan to tackle existing debt together. Prioritize high-interest debt and explore debt payoff strategies.

- Investment Strategy: Discuss your investment risk tolerance and determine an investment strategy that aligns with your shared goals.

Building a United Financial Front:

- Open Joint Accounts: Consider opening joint checking and savings accounts for shared expenses and joint financial goals.

- Shared Financial Responsibility: Decide how you'll handle bills and everyday expenses. Will you split them equally, or will one partner manage specific costs?

- Emergency Fund: Build a joint emergency fund to cover unexpected expenses and avoid financial stress.

Tools for Success:

Several tools can facilitate financial planning and communication as a couple:

- Budgeting Apps: Utilize budgeting apps designed for couples to track joint income and expenses, set shared financial goals, and monitor progress.

- Financial Planning Software: Consider using financial planning software to model your future financial situation and make informed decisions.

- Financial Advisor: Consult with a financial advisor to receive personalized guidance and develop a financial plan tailored to your specific circumstances and goals.

Remember: Financial situations and goals can evolve over time. Regularly review your joint financial plan, have open discussions about any changes, and adjust your strategies as needed.

Beyond Finances:

While financial compatibility is important, a fulfilling relationship goes beyond money. Nurture other aspects of your partnership like communication, trust, and shared values.

Building a life together with a shared vision for financial security strengthens your partnership and sets the foundation for a bright and prosperous future. By following these tips and fostering open communication, you and your life partner can achieve financial freedom and live the life you both dream of!

Chapter 14: Living Below Your Means - The Master Key to Financial Freedom

Congratulations! Throughout this guide, you've unlocked valuable tools and strategies for taking control of your finances. This final chapter focuses on a cornerstone principle for financial success – living below your means.

What Does It Mean to Live Below Your Means?

Living below your means simply means spending less than you earn. It's not about deprivation, but about making conscious choices to prioritize your financial well-being. Here's the core principle:

- Income - Essential Expenses - Debt Payments = Savings & Investments

By ensuring your income consistently exceeds your essential expenses and debt obligations, you create space for savings and investments. This is the foundation for building wealth and achieving your financial goals.

Why is Living Below Your Means Important?

Here are some compelling reasons to embrace this approach:

- Financial Security: Living below your means allows you to build an emergency fund, pay off debt, and save for the future. This financial security reduces stress and empowers you to make choices based on your long-term goals, not short-term impulses.

- Freedom from Debt: The cycle of debt can be suffocating. Living below your means allows you to prioritize debt repayment and ultimately achieve financial freedom.

- Achieving Financial Goals: Whether it's a dream vacation, a down payment on a house, or early retirement, living below your means allows you to save and invest towards achieving your financial aspirations.

Living Below Means Doesn't Mean Living Miserably

It's a misconception that living below your means equates to a joyless existence. It's about making smart choices and prioritizing what truly matters. Here are some tips:

- Differentiate Needs vs. Wants: Learn to distinguish between essential needs (housing, food, healthcare) and fleeting desires. Prioritize needs and be mindful of impulse purchases.

- Embrace Frugal Living: Frugal living isn't about deprivation, but about maximizing the value you get for your money. Explore cost-saving alternatives for everyday expenses.

- **Find Free or Low-Cost Fun:** There's a world of activities and entertainment options that don't require breaking the bank. Explore parks, libraries, museums with free admission days, or outdoor activities.
- **Cook at Home More Often:** Eating out can significantly impact your budget. Cooking at home is generally cheaper and healthier.
- **Challenge Yourself:** Set a savings challenge and see how much you can save in a specific period. This can be a fun and motivating way to live below your means.

Living Below Your Means is a Journey, Not a Destination

There will be times when you splurge or your expenses might increase. Don't be discouraged. The key is to recommit to your goals and get back on track with your spending plan.

Remember: Living below your means is a powerful tool that empowers you to take control of your financial destiny. By adopting this approach, you can build a secure financial future and unlock the door to the life you've always dreamed of.

Congratulations! You've completed this guide to budgeting and financial wellness. By applying the principles and strategies outlined in these chapters, you're well on your way to achieving financial freedom and living a fulfilling life!

What are your thoughts?:

Chapter 15: Building Your Financial Fortress - Creating Multiple Streams of Income

Congratulations! You've mastered budgeting, explored investment strategies, and learned to live below your means. These are all foundational pillars for financial security. Now, let's delve into the exciting realm of multiplying your income and building wealth through creating multiple streams of revenue.

Why Multiple Income Streams?

Relying solely on one paycheck can leave you vulnerable to unexpected events like job loss or economic downturns. Diversifying your income streams creates a financial safety net and accelerates your wealth-building journey. Here are some reasons to consider multiple income sources:

- Increased Financial Security: Multiple income streams provide a financial buffer. If one source falters, the others can help you weather the storm.

- Faster Path to Financial Goals: The more income you generate, the faster you can save for your goals, pay off debt, or invest for the future.

- Freedom and Flexibility: Additional income streams can provide financial independence and the freedom to pursue your passions or work less if desired.

Exploring Your Income Potential:

Here are some ideas to spark your creativity and help you identify potential income streams:

- Develop Your Skills and Expertise: Can you leverage your existing skills or knowledge to consult, freelance, or teach online courses?

- The Gig Economy: Explore platforms offering freelance work, online tutoring, or task-based gigs that fit your schedule and skillset.

- Passion Projects: Can you monetize a hobby or passion? Consider selling crafts, creating online content, or offering niche services related to your interests.

- Rental Income: Do you have a spare room or a vacation property? Renting it out can generate passive income.

- Investing: While not entirely passive, investing in dividend-paying stocks, real estate investment trusts (REITs), or creating a peer-to-peer lending portfolio can generate ongoing income.

Example: Building a Side Business with Social Media and Etsy

Let's explore how someone with a passion for handmade jewelry can create a side business and generate additional income. Here are some steps involved:

1. Refine Your Skills and Products: Focus on creating high-quality, unique jewelry that caters to a specific audience.
2. Develop Your Brand: Craft a brand name and logo that reflects your style and target audience.
3. Leverage Social Media: Create engaging profiles on platforms like Instagram, Facebook, or Pinterest. Showcase your work, share behind-the-scenes glimpses, and interact with potential customers. Utilize eye-catching product photos and videos to capture attention.
4. Build an Online Store: Open an Etsy shop to list and sell your products. Etsy offers a user-friendly platform to reach a wide audience of potential buyers.
5. Explore Online Marketplaces: Consider selling on additional online marketplaces like Amazon Handmade or Shopify, depending on your target market and product type.
6. Run Targeted Ads: Social media platforms and Etsy offer advertising options to reach a wider audience and attract potential customers. Start with a small budget and track the results to see if it yields a positive return on investment.
7. Customer Service: Provide excellent customer service to build trust and encourage repeat business. Respond promptly to inquiries, offer clear return policies, and ensure a smooth buying experience.

Remember: Building a successful side business takes time and effort. Be patient, experiment with different marketing strategies, and continuously adapt based on what works for you.

Things to Consider:

- Time Commitment: Evaluate the time commitment required for your side business and ensure it aligns with your existing schedule and priorities.
- Investment Costs: There might be upfront costs for materials, tools, setting up an online store, or running advertisements.
- Taxes: Research the tax implications of your side business income and factor them into your calculations.

Building a Sustainable Income Ecosystem:

The key to success is creating a sustainable system of income streams that complement your lifestyle and financial goals. Here are some additional tips:

- **Focus on Your Strengths:** Capitalize on your existing skills and knowledge when exploring new income opportunities.

- **Balance is Key:** While generating additional income is important, avoid neglecting your well-being or primary job responsibilities.

- **Embrace Continuous Learning:** The world of work is constantly evolving. Stay updated on new skills and explore opportunities to expand your income potential.

Remember: Financial freedom isn't just about how much you earn, but also about managing your expenses wisely. Combine creating multiple income streams with your budgeting skills and sound financial planning for maximum

Chapter 16: Retirement Rendezvous - Living Off 4% and Thriving in Your Golden Years

Congratulations on reaching retirement! After years of hard work and careful financial planning, it's time to enjoy the rewards and make the most of this new phase of life. This chapter delves into the renowned "4% rule" and offers strategies to help you manage your retirement savings wisely for a fulfilling retirement.

Understanding the 4% Rule: Your Retirement Income Roadmap

The 4% rule serves as a reliable guideline for retirees to determine a sustainable annual withdrawal rate from their retirement savings. Here's how it works:

Imagine you have saved $1.2 million for retirement. According to the 4% rule, you can withdraw approximately $48,000 (4% of $1.2 million) in the first year of retirement. Subsequent withdrawals should be adjusted for inflation to maintain your purchasing power over time.

Important Considerations

While the 4% rule provides a useful framework, several factors can influence its effectiveness:

- Life Expectancy: With longer life expectancies, your retirement savings need to last longer. Consider how long you expect to live when deciding on withdrawal rates.

  Market Volatility: Fluctuations in the stock market can impact your retirement portfolio. Withdrawing during market downturns may deplete your savings more quickly.

  Retirement Lifestyle: Your desired lifestyle in retirement — whether it includes extensive travel, hobbies, or other pursuits — will affect how much you need to withdraw annually.

Strategies for Ensuring a Secure Retirement

To ensure your retirement savings endure throughout your golden years, consider these essential strategies:

Delay Social Security: Delaying your Social Security benefits can increase your monthly payments, providing a higher income stream later in retirement.

Healthcare Planning: Factor potential healthcare costs into your retirement budget. Health savings accounts (HSAs) and long-term care insurance can help manage these expenses effectively.

Debt Management: Aim to enter retirement without significant debt obligations. High debt payments can strain your retirement income and limit financial flexibility.

Spending Monitoring: Regularly monitor your retirement expenses and adjust your withdrawal rate as needed. Flexibility in spending is crucial to adapting to unexpected changes.

Self-Banking: Financing Purchases with Savings

This approach encourages treating your savings like a personal bank to finance larger purchases. Here's the idea:

- Set Aside Savings: Allocate a portion of your income regularly to build a dedicated savings pool.
- Simulate Loan Payments: Instead of credit card debt, calculate a monthly "payment" amount as if you were financing the purchase from your savings.
- Charge Yourself Interest: Consider adding a small "interest charge" to your monthly payment, mimicking traditional loan terms.

Benefits:

- Reduced Interest Costs: Avoid high credit card interest rates by financing purchases with your own money.
- Forced Savings: The "loan payment" structure encourages consistent savings.
- Sense of Ownership: Paying yourself back builds a sense of accomplishment and ownership over your purchase.

Important Considerations:

- Discipline Required: Sticking to the "payment" plan requires discipline and delayed gratification.
- Opportunity Cost: Savings used for purchases may miss out on potential investment returns.
- Limited Borrowing Power: This approach relies on existing savings, unlike credit that offers temporary access to larger sums.

Alternatives for Financing Purchases:

- Traditional Loans: May offer lower interest rates for larger purchases compared to credit cards.
- Savings Plans: Some retailers offer 0% interest financing for specific periods.

- **Responsible Credit Card Use:** For planned purchases, utilizing a credit card with a rewards program might be advantageous.

Remember:

This approach focuses on financial discipline and avoiding high-interest debt. It's important to carefully evaluate your financial situation and needs before implementing this strategy.

Focus on Fulfillment in Retirement

Retirement isn't just about finances; it's about enriching your life in meaningful ways:

Pursue Passions: Engage in hobbies, travel, or pursue interests you didn't have time for during your working years.

Maintain Social Connections: Strong relationships with friends and family are vital for emotional well-being in retirement.

Continual Learning: Embrace lifelong learning by taking courses, exploring new subjects, or acquiring new skills.

Give Back: Volunteer or mentor others to contribute to your community and find purpose in retirement.

Notes:

Chapter 17: Simplified Budgeting with Practical Rules

In this chapter, we're diving into practical budgeting strategies that apply to real-world scenarios. It's crucial to scrutinize financial advice to ensure it aligns with your own circumstances. Let's break down how to implement these principles effectively.

Understanding Your Take-Home Pay

Begin by examining your paystub to determine your actual cash-in-hand income. For instance, in 2024, the average income is approximately $59,849 per year. After accounting for deductions like healthcare, 401k contributions, and taxes — which typically amount to around 28-35% — a single person might have roughly $3,000 per month available for expenses.

Living by Rules That Govern

Rule 1: The 70/20/10 Rule

You may have encountered the 70/20/10 rule before, but let's break it down practically. This rule suggests allocating:

70% of your income to living expenses such as rent, utilities, transportation, and entertainment.

- 20% to debt repayment.

- 10% to savings and investments.

Applying the 70/20/10 Rule

For example, if $3,000 is your monthly cash-in-hand:

70% (or $2,100) should cover living expenses. Breakdowns like the recommended 28% for rent might seem unrealistic if your actual rent is higher, such as $900. This rule isn't about strict numbers but about setting limits. If you exceed 28% on rent, adjust other categories accordingly to stay within your overall budget.

20% (or $600) is dedicated to debt repayment. If your current debt obligations are less than this amount, it's an opportunity to accelerate debt reduction or allocate towards other financial goals.

-10% (or $300) should be set aside for savings and investments. Always prioritize paying yourself first to build a financial safety net and prepare for future needs.

Practical Tips for Managing Expenses

Transportation: Limit car expenses to 15% of your income, including insurance. Consider budget-friendly options when purchasing a vehicle.

Utilities: Control utility costs through energy-saving practices and careful budgeting.

Groceries: Manage food expenses by aiming for cost-effective meals, roughly $3 per meal, totaling around $270 per month.

Flexibility and Adjustments

These budget rules provide a framework but allow for flexibility. Adjust categories based on your personal circumstances and priorities. For instance, reallocating funds towards unexpected expenses like birthdays or emergencies demonstrates practical flexibility within the budget structure.

Investing in Your Future

Always prioritize savings and investments. This 10% allocation ensures financial growth and security over time. Whether for retirement or unforeseen emergencies, this fund serves as a crucial safety net.

Conclusion

By adhering to these structured yet flexible budgeting principles, you can stabilize your finances and focus on achieving your life goals. Regularly review and adjust your budget with a partner or trusted advisor to stay on track. Remember, these principles are applicable regardless of income level, providing a solid foundation for financial stability and future growth.

Embrace these guidelines as a disciplined approach to managing your finances, ensuring you're prepared for whatever life may bring.

Give me three Disciplines for money?

Hint: what do you think they are!

Chapter 18: Balancing Work and Lifestyle

In our daily lives, work and lifestyle often dominate our priorities. We observe colleagues with their fancy cars and exotic travels, and we wonder about their stability. However, life can throw unexpected challenges, like illness or job loss, even when we feel secure. That's why it's crucial to align our work and lifestyle choices with our income levels.

Prioritizing Stability Over Appearances

Don't be swayed by others' flashy purchases. Instead, focus on preparing for tomorrow. For instance, someone who buys a luxurious car today could struggle if they lose their job tomorrow. It's essential to continuously develop skills that enhance your value in society. This doesn't necessarily mean aiming for a CEO position; rather, it involves becoming proficient in managing finances, maintaining property, and safeguarding well-being.

Investing in Your Health and Skills

Taking care of yourself is fundamental. Adopting a balanced diet and regular exercise routine — even 30 minutes to an hour, three times a week — can significantly enhance your well-being and future outlook. While these habits may not always be enjoyable, they contribute to long-term happiness and stability.

Planning for the Future: The 3, 5, and 10 Year Plans

3 Year Plan:

Start by evaluating your current career path. Assess whether it offers growth opportunities or if you need to pivot towards a different field. Research potential jobs and their requirements, including skills and education. Seek mentors and attend relevant seminars to broaden your network and knowledge base.

Managing Your Daily Routine

The traditional 8-hour divisions of sleep, work, and personal time might not always fit practical realities. Adjustments, like reducing sleep slightly or blending family time with skill-building activities, can make your schedule more manageable while keeping your goals in focus.

5 Year Plan:

Align your five-year plan with your career ambitions and financial goals. Evaluate progress regularly and adjust your strategies as needed. Seek feedback from mentors to refine your approach and stay on track towards achieving your desired lifestyle and financial stability.

10 Year Destination:

Look ahead to where you want to be in a decade, considering financial independence, lifestyle enhancements, personal freedom, and career milestones. Your plans should be adaptable to life's changes while holding yourself accountable for achieving set objectives. Life's journey will have its challenges, but persistence and continuous learning are key. Embrace setbacks as learning opportunities, adjust your plans as necessary, and remain focused on your long-term aspirations. By following these principles and maintaining flexibility, you can build a stable and fulfilling future. Remember, the path to success may be winding, but each step forward brings you closer to the life you envision.

Chapter 19: Daily Requirements of Simple Budgeting

One of the most critical habits you can develop for financial success is daily tracking of your income and expenses. Whether you choose to use budgeting software like YNAB or a simpler method, consistency is key. Here's how to implement and maintain this practice effectively:

Daily Tracking and Entry

Every transaction, from grocery purchases to gas fill-ups, should be promptly recorded in your budgeting tool or spreadsheet. This ensures that every dollar has a designated purpose and helps you stay accountable to your financial goals. For example, if you go out to a bar, enter the expenditure into your budget immediately upon returning home.

Weekly Review and Adjustment

Allocate time each week—perhaps on Friday night or before your day off—to review and reconcile your budget. This regular check-in allows you to balance your budget, reallocate funds as needed, and ensure that your spending aligns with your financial plan. It's beneficial to involve your partner in this process to foster transparency and shared financial responsibility.

Tracking Variable Expenses

Variable costs such as utilities and subscriptions require careful monitoring. Stay informed about changes in oil prices, electricity rates, or subscription fees through regular updates and adjust your budget accordingly. This proactive approach helps anticipate and manage financial fluctuations.

Building Discipline and Flexibility

Consistent tracking and weekly reviews build financial discipline. This habit reinforces the rules you set for yourself and strengthens your commitment to achieving financial goals. Moreover, it allows you to adapt quickly to unexpected expenses or changes in income without derailing your financial plan. If you ever need to use credit cards due to unforeseen circumstances, prioritize paying off the balance swiftly to avoid accumulating high-interest debt.

Personal Testimony and Growth

It took me three months to establish this disciplined approach, but over nine years, it has transformed my financial trajectory. Starting as a factory worker, I've grown my net worth to $360,000 and advanced to a six-figure job. This journey has been challenging but immensely rewarding since embracing financial principles and continuous learning.

Notes:

Paying Yourself First:

Always allocate a portion of your income to savings or investments—ideally, 10%. This practice, known as paying yourself first, ensures that you prioritize your future financial security. If 10% seems daunting initially, start with 5% and gradually increase as your financial habits strengthen. Automating this savings process reinforces discipline and helps you consistently build towards your long-term goals. By integrating daily tracking, weekly reviews, and disciplined savings habits into your routine, you create a robust financial framework. This method not only empowers you to manage your money effectively but also prepares you for unexpected challenges and opportunities. Remember, financial success is a journey that requires commitment, adaptability, and a steadfast belief in the principles that guide your financial decisions.

Notes:

A Heartfelt Thank You

Dear Reader,

Thank you from the bottom of my heart for purchasing this book. I truly hope it serves as a valuable guide on your journey to financial freedom.

This book delves deep into the world of saving, investing, and building wealth. I encourage you to explore the recommendations and ideas presented, and tailor them to your unique situation.

There's No Magic Formula:

This book isn't about a secret million-dollar trick. It's about fostering a **discipline** that brings stability and control to your finances.

By applying the principles outlined here, you can build a solid foundation for a secure and prosperous future.

Thank You Again, and Best Wishes!

May your path be filled with financial well-being and happiness.

Sincerely,

Timothy Snyder

www.ingramcontent.com/pod-product-compliance
Lightning Source LLC
Chambersburg PA
CBHW072021230526
45479CB00008B/316